INNOVATE TO ELEVATE

I0427269

UNLEASHING ENTREPRENEURIAL SUCCESS

NANCY BARLOW

TABLE OF CONTENT

INTRODUCTION

In a world characterized by rapid technological advancements, shifting market landscapes, and ever-evolving consumer demands, the pursuit of entrepreneurial success demands more than just traditional business acumen. It requires a relentless commitment to innovation—an ability to adapt, evolve, and transform ideas into impactful solutions. Welcome to "Innovate to Elevate: Unleashing Entrepreneurial Success," a groundbreaking manifesto crafted to empower aspiring and seasoned entrepreneurs alike on their journey towards sustainable prosperity.

In this compelling exploration of innovation in entrepreneurship, we delve deep into the core principles, strategies, and mindsets that drive success in today's dynamic business environment. Drawing from a diverse tapestry of real-world examples, case studies, and expert insights, this book serves as a comprehensive roadmap for navigating the complexities of entrepreneurship in the 21st century.

At its heart, "Innovate to Elevate" challenges conventional wisdom and dares entrepreneurs to break free from the shackles of conformity. It celebrates the audacity of dreaming big and the courage to pursue uncharted territories. Through a fusion of inspiration and practicality, readers will uncover invaluable strategies for identifying market opportunities, fostering creativity, and harnessing the power of innovation to carve out their niche in competitive industries.

Moreover, this book transcends mere theory, offering actionable advice and tangible frameworks that readers can immediately apply to their entrepreneurial endeavors. Whether you're a budding startup founder seeking to disrupt industries or an established business leader aiming to stay ahead of the curve, "Innovate to Elevate" equips you with the tools, insights, and inspiration needed to thrive in an era defined by constant change and disruption.

As we embark on this transformative journey together, prepare to challenge the status quo, embrace uncertainty, and unlock the boundless potential of innovation. The time to elevate your entrepreneurial journey is now.

CHAPTER 1:

UNDERSTANDING THE

INNOVATION

IMPERATIVE

The landscape of entrepreneurship has undergone a seismic shift in recent years, propelled by technological advancements, changing consumer preferences, and globalization. In this chapter, we delve into the essence of innovation as the cornerstone of entrepreneurial success, exploring its significance in navigating today's dynamic business environment.

The Evolution of Entrepreneurship in the Digital Age:

We begin by tracing the evolution of entrepreneurship from its traditional roots to the digital age. The rise of technology has democratized access to markets, lowered barriers to entry, and revolutionized business models. We examine how this transformation has necessitated a shift in mindset, where innovation becomes not just a choice but a survival imperative for entrepreneurs striving to stay relevant and competitive.

Why Innovation is the Key to Long-Term Success:

Here, we explore the intrinsic link between innovation and long-term success in entrepreneurship. Drawing on research and real-world examples, we highlight how companies that prioritize innovation consistently outperform their competitors, adapt to changing market conditions, and sustain growth over time. Moreover, we discuss the risks of complacency and the perils of failing to innovate in an era defined by disruption.

Exploring the Intersection of Creativity and Problem-Solving:

At the core of innovation lies the synergy between creativity and problem-solving. We delve into the cognitive processes behind creativity, examining how entrepreneurs can cultivate a mindset that fosters divergent thinking, experimentation, and the exploration of unconventional solutions. Moreover, we discuss the importance of identifying and understanding customer pain points as catalysts for innovation, emphasizing the need for empathy and user-centric design in problem-solving.

Understanding the innovation imperative is not merely about embracing change; it's about embracing the limitless possibilities that arise from challenging the status quo. In this chapter, we lay the foundation for a deeper exploration of innovation as a driving force behind entrepreneurial success, setting the stage for practical strategies and insights to follow in subsequent chapters.

- The Evolution of Entrepreneurship in the Digital Age

The dawn of the digital age has redefined the landscape of entrepreneurship, reshaping traditional notions of business and paving the way for unprecedented opportunities. This section explores the transformative journey of entrepreneurship from its historical roots to the dynamic ecosystem of the digital era.

Historical Perspectives:

The historical context of entrepreneurship spans centuries, evolving alongside shifts in economic systems, technological advancements, and societal structures. Tracing its origins from ancient trade routes and mercantile ventures to the Industrial Revolution and the rise of capitalism provides valuable insights into the development and significance of entrepreneurship throughout history.

1. Ancient Trade Routes:

Entrepreneurship can be traced back to ancient civilizations where traders and merchants engaged in commercial activities along established trade routes. From the Silk Road in Asia to the Mediterranean Sea in Europe, these trade networks facilitated the exchange of goods, ideas, and culture, laying the foundation for early entrepreneurial endeavors. Merchants played a pivotal role in connecting distant regions, fostering economic growth, and fueling innovation through trade.

2. Mercantile Ventures:

During the middle Ages and Renaissance period, the emergence of mercantilism led to the rise of merchant guilds and trading companies. These organizations provided a framework for entrepreneurs to collaborate, share resources, and mitigate risks associated with long-distance trade. The expansion of global trade routes, exploration, and colonization further spurred entrepreneurial activity, as merchants sought new markets and opportunities for profit.

3. Industrial Revolution:

The Industrial Revolution marked a pivotal moment in the history of entrepreneurship, as technological innovations transformed manufacturing processes and spurred urbanization. Entrepreneurs played a central role in driving industrialization, investing in machinery, infrastructure, and labor to mass-produce goods. The rise of factories, steam power, and mechanization revolutionized production methods, leading to unprecedented economic growth and social change.

4. Rise of Capitalism:

The advent of capitalism in the 18th and 19th centuries provided fertile ground for entrepreneurial activity to flourish. Capitalism, characterized by private ownership of the means of production and free market competition, incentivized innovation and risk-taking. Entrepreneurs seized opportunities in emerging industries such as textiles, transportation, and finance, driving economic expansion and wealth creation. The rise of industrial titans, such as Andrew Carnegie and John D. Rockefeller, exemplified the entrepreneurial spirit of the era, as individuals built vast empires through ingenuity, ambition, and strategic vision.

5. **Innovation and Technological Advancements:**

Throughout the 20th and 21st centuries, entrepreneurship has continued to evolve alongside rapid technological advancements and globalization. From the invention of the automobile and the airplane to the advent of the internet and digital revolution, entrepreneurs have leveraged innovation to disrupt industries, create new markets, and drive economic growth. The tech industry, in particular, has become a hotbed of entrepreneurial activity, as startups and innovators harness the power of technology to solve complex problems and shape the future.

The historical context of entrepreneurship reflects its enduring relevance and significance in driving economic progress and societal change. From ancient trade routes to the digital age, entrepreneurs have played a central role in shaping the course of human history, demonstrating resilience, creativity, and adaptability in the face of challenges and opportunities. As we look to the future, entrepreneurship remains a powerful force for innovation, empowerment, and economic development, shaping the world we live in and inspiring generations to come.

The Digital Revolution:

Digital technologies have fundamentally transformed the entrepreneurial landscape, empowering agile startups to challenge established incumbents and disrupt entire industries in unprecedented ways. This comprehensive shift has been facilitated by several key factors:

1. **Accessibility and Affordability:**

Digital technologies have democratized entrepreneurship by making tools, resources, and information more accessible and affordable than ever before. Cloud computing, software as a service (SaaS) platforms, and open-source software enable startups to leverage powerful tools and infrastructure without significant upfront investment. This accessibility lowers barriers to entry, allowing entrepreneurs to launch innovative ventures with minimal capital and resources.

2. **Global Reach and Market Access:**

The internet has connected the world like never before, providing startups with unprecedented global reach and market access. E-commerce platforms, social media, and digital marketing channels enable entrepreneurs to reach potential customers across borders and time zones, bypassing traditional barriers to entry. This global connectivity allows startups to scale rapidly and compete on a level playing field with established incumbents, regardless of their size or location.

3. Disintermediation and Direct-to-Consumer Models:

Digital technologies have facilitated disintermediation, enabling startups to bypass traditional intermediaries and connect directly with customers. Direct-to-consumer (DTC) models leverage e-commerce platforms, online marketplaces, and social media channels to eliminate middlemen and offer products and services directly to consumers. By cutting out distributors, wholesalers, and retailers, startups can capture more value and deliver a superior customer experience, disrupting traditional supply chains and distribution channels.

4. Data-Driven Decision-Making:

Digital technologies have enabled startups to leverage data analytics, machine learning, and artificial intelligence to make informed, data-driven decisions. By collecting and analyzing vast amounts of data, startups can gain insights into customer behavior, market trends, and competitive dynamics, allowing them to iterate quickly, optimize strategies, and stay ahead of the curve. This data-driven approach gives startups a competitive edge, enabling them to identify untapped opportunities and respond rapidly to changing market conditions.

5. Agile Development and Iterative Processes:

Digital technologies have facilitated agile development methodologies, enabling startups to iterate quickly, adapt to feedback, and pivot in response to market demands. Agile methodologies, such as scrum and lean startup, prioritize rapid prototyping, experimentation, and continuous improvement, allowing startups to validate assumptions, test hypotheses, and refine their products or services iteratively. This iterative approach minimizes risk, maximizes learning, and accelerates time-to-market, giving startups a strategic advantage over slower-moving incumbents.

6. Innovation and Disruption:

Digital technologies have catalyzed innovation and disruption across industries, challenging established incumbents and reshaping competitive dynamics. Startups leverage emerging technologies, such as artificial intelligence, blockchain, and the Internet of Things (IoT), to develop disruptive business models and redefine industry norms. By embracing innovation and taking calculated risks, startups can capitalize on market inefficiencies, address unmet needs, and carve out a niche in crowded markets, disrupting incumbents and capturing market share in the process.

Digital technologies have facilitated new forms of entrepreneurship, enabling agile startups to challenge established incumbents and disrupt entire industries. By leveraging accessibility, global reach, disintermediation, data-driven decision-making, agile development, and innovation, startups can harness the power of digital technologies to drive growth, create value, and reshape the future of business. As digital transformation continues to accelerate, the entrepreneurial landscape will continue to evolve, creating new opportunities for innovation, disruption, and success.

Globalization and Market Dynamics:

Globalization has profoundly reshaped market dynamics, presenting both opportunities and challenges for entrepreneurs in an increasingly interconnected world. Understanding the implications of globalization is essential for entrepreneurs seeking to navigate the complexities of global markets and capitalize on emerging trends. Here, we comprehensively discuss the opportunities and challenges faced by entrepreneurs in the context of globalization:

Opportunities:

1. Access to Global Markets:

Globalization has expanded access to international markets, providing entrepreneurs with unprecedented opportunities to reach customers worldwide. Advances in transportation, communication, and e-commerce have made it easier for startups to sell their products or services globally, regardless of their size or location.

Entrepreneurs can leverage digital platforms, online marketplaces, and social media channels to connect with customers across borders and time zones, enabling them to scale rapidly and compete on a global scale.

2. Diverse Talent Pool:

Globalization has facilitated the movement of talent across borders, allowing entrepreneurs to access a diverse pool of skilled workers, innovators, and collaborators from around the world. By leveraging remote work arrangements, freelance platforms, and international partnerships, entrepreneurs can tap into talent pools with diverse backgrounds, expertise, and perspectives. This diversity fosters creativity, innovation, and cross-cultural collaboration, enabling startups to develop more innovative solutions and better serve global customers.

3. Supply Chain Optimization:

Globalization has enabled entrepreneurs to optimize their supply chains by sourcing materials, components, and labor from locations with cost advantages or specialized expertise. By leveraging global sourcing strategies, entrepreneurs can reduce production costs, improve product quality, and enhance supply chain resilience. Additionally, advances in logistics and transportation infrastructure have made it easier for startups to manage complex supply chains and streamline operations, enabling them to deliver products to customers more efficiently and effectively.

4. Strategic Partnerships and Alliances:

Globalization has created opportunities for entrepreneurs to form strategic partnerships and alliances with companies, organizations, and institutions from around the world. By collaborating with international partners, entrepreneurs can access new markets, technologies, and resources, enabling them to accelerate growth and expand their reach.

Strategic partnerships can also provide startups with access to capital, expertise, and distribution channels, helping them overcome barriers to entry and compete more effectively in global markets.

Challenges:

1. Increased Competition:

Globalization has intensified competition in many industries, as startups face competition not only from local competitors but also from international rivals. Entrepreneurs must contend with competitors who may have greater resources, brand recognition, and market presence, making it challenging to differentiate their offerings and capture market share. Additionally, globalization has lowered barriers to entry, allowing new competitors to enter markets more easily, further increasing competitive pressures for entrepreneurs.

2. Regulatory Complexity:

Globalization has introduced regulatory complexity for entrepreneurs operating in multiple jurisdictions, as they must navigate diverse legal frameworks, taxation regimes, and compliance requirements. Entrepreneurs must stay abreast of regulatory changes and ensure compliance with local laws and regulations in each market they operate in, which can be time-consuming, costly, and resource-intensive. Failure to comply with regulatory requirements can expose startups to legal risks, reputational damage, and financial penalties, making regulatory compliance a significant challenge for entrepreneurs in a globalized world.

3. Cultural and Linguistic Differences:

Globalization has highlighted the importance of understanding and navigating cultural and linguistic differences when conducting business in international markets. Entrepreneurs must be sensitive to cultural norms, values, and preferences when marketing products or services to customers from diverse backgrounds. Additionally, language barriers can pose communication challenges and hinder effective collaboration with international partners, suppliers, and customers. Entrepreneurs must invest in cross-cultural training, localization efforts, and language support to overcome these challenges and build meaningful relationships in global markets.

4. Supply Chain Disruptions:

Globalization has increased the interconnectedness of supply chains, making them more vulnerable to disruptions from natural disasters, geopolitical events, and global crises. Entrepreneurs must anticipate and mitigate supply chain risks by diversifying sourcing strategies, building redundancy into supply chains, and developing contingency plans for managing disruptions. Supply chain disruptions can disrupt production, delay deliveries, and impact customer satisfaction, posing significant challenges for entrepreneurs in maintaining operational continuity and meeting customer demand.

Globalization presents both opportunities and challenges for entrepreneurs in an increasingly interconnected world. While globalization expands access to global markets, talent pools, and strategic partnerships, it also intensifies competition, regulatory complexity, and supply chain risks. Entrepreneurs must navigate these challenges effectively by leveraging digital technologies, fostering cross-cultural understanding, and building resilient, agile organizations capable of thriving in the dynamic global marketplace. By embracing globalization as a driver of innovation and growth, entrepreneurs can position themselves to succeed in an increasingly interconnected and competitive world.

Emerging Trends and Future Outlook:

Cutting-edge technologies and shifting societal values are fundamentally reshaping the entrepreneurial landscape, ushering in a new era of innovation, disruption, and opportunity. These transformative forces are driving significant changes in how entrepreneurs start, grow, and scale their ventures, as well as how they address emerging challenges and capitalize on emerging trends. Here, we comprehensively discuss how cutting-edge technologies and shifting societal values are reshaping the entrepreneurial landscape:

1. **Technological Advancements:**

a. **Artificial Intelligence (AI) and Machine Learning:** AI and machine learning technologies are revolutionizing how entrepreneurs analyze data, automate processes, and make decisions. From predictive analytics and personalized recommendations to autonomous systems and natural language processing, AI enables startups to develop innovative products and services that anticipate and adapt to customer needs.

b. **Internet of Things (IoT):** The IoT is transforming industries by connecting physical devices, sensors, and objects to the Internet, enabling real-time monitoring, control, and optimization of systems and processes. Entrepreneurs are leveraging IoT technologies to create smart products, optimize supply chains, and improve operational efficiency across diverse sectors, from manufacturing and logistics to healthcare and agriculture.

c. **Blockchain and Cryptocurrency**: Blockchain technology is disrupting traditional business models by providing secure, transparent, and decentralized systems for recording and verifying transactions. Entrepreneurs are exploring applications of blockchain and cryptocurrency in areas such as supply chain management, digital identity, and financial services, creating new opportunities for innovation and value creation.

d. **Augmented Reality (AR) and Virtual Reality (VR)**: AR and VR technologies are blurring the lines between the physical and digital worlds, enabling immersive experiences and interactive storytelling. Entrepreneurs are leveraging AR and VR to create engaging marketing campaigns, virtual product demonstrations, and interactive training programs, enhancing customer engagement and driving brand loyalty.

e. **Quantum Computing and Edge Computing:**
Quantum computing and edge computing are poised to revolutionize computing infrastructure, enabling faster processing speeds, enhanced security, and greater scalability. Entrepreneurs are exploring applications of quantum computing and edge computing in areas such as optimization, simulation, and cyber security, unlocking new possibilities for innovation and disruption.

2. Shifting Societal Values:

a. **Sustainability and Environmental** Responsibility: Shifting societal values toward sustainability and environmental responsibility are driving demand for eco-friendly products, renewable energy solutions, and sustainable business practices. Entrepreneurs are responding to these trends by developing innovative solutions to address environmental challenges, such as carbon capture technology, sustainable packaging, and circular economy models.

b. **Diversity, Equity, and Inclusion**: There is growing awareness and emphasis on diversity, equity, and inclusion in the entrepreneurial landscape, as stakeholders demand greater representation and equality. Entrepreneurs are prioritizing diversity in hiring, fostering inclusive cultures, and championing social justice causes to build more equitable and inclusive organizations.

c. **Wellness and Mental Health:** The importance of wellness and mental health is gaining recognition in society, driving demand for products and services that promote physical, mental, and emotional well-being. Entrepreneurs are developing innovative solutions in areas such as telemedicine, mindfulness apps, and workplace wellness programs to address the growing need for holistic health solutions.

d. **Remote Work and Digital Nomadism**: The COVID-19 pandemic has accelerated the adoption of remote work and digital nomadism, reshaping how entrepreneurs and employees work and collaborate. Entrepreneurs are embracing remote work tools, virtual collaboration platforms, and flexible work arrangements to enable remote teams to work efficiently and effectively from anywhere in the world.

e. **Ethical Consumerism and Conscious Consumption**: There is a growing trend toward ethical consumerism and conscious consumption, with consumers seeking products and brands that align with their values and beliefs. Entrepreneurs are responding by adopting transparent and ethical business practices, sourcing sustainable materials, and supporting social causes to appeal to socially conscious consumers.

Cutting-edge technologies and shifting societal values are reshaping the entrepreneurial landscape in profound ways, creating new opportunities for innovation, disruption, and positive impact. Entrepreneurs who embrace these transformative forces and leverage them to address emerging challenges and capitalize on emerging trends will be well-positioned to succeed in the dynamic and rapidly evolving entrepreneurial ecosystem. By harnessing the power of cutting-edge technologies and aligning with shifting societal values, entrepreneurs can drive meaningful change, create sustainable businesses, and shape the future of entrepreneurship.

The evolution of entrepreneurship in the digital age is a testament to the resilience and ingenuity of human enterprise. As we reflect on the journey thus far, it becomes evident that the digital revolution has not only transformed how we do business but also redefined what it means to be an entrepreneur in the 21st century. In the chapters that follow, we will delve deeper into the principles, strategies, and mindsets that drive entrepreneurial success in this dynamic and ever-evolving landscape.

- Why Innovation is the Key to Long-Term Success

Innovation is not merely a buzzword; it's a fundamental driver of long-term success in entrepreneurship. This section delves into the myriad reasons why innovation is indispensable for businesses aiming to thrive amidst constant change and disruption.

Adaptation to Changing Market Dynamics:

One of the primary reasons why innovation is crucial for long-term success is its role in helping businesses adapt to changing market dynamics. Markets are in a constant state of flux, influenced by technological advancements, shifting consumer preferences, and global trends. Innovators are better positioned to anticipate and respond to these changes, allowing them to seize opportunities and mitigate risks effectively.

Competitive Advantage and Market Differentiation:

Innovation enables businesses to differentiate themselves from competitors and gain a competitive advantage. Whether through product innovation, process optimization, or business model innovation, companies that innovate stand out in crowded markets. By offering unique value propositions and addressing unmet needs, innovators can attract and retain customers, command premium prices, and capture market share.

Sustainable Growth and Resilience:

Innovation fosters sustainable growth by fueling continuous improvement and renewal. Businesses that innovate are better equipped to stay ahead of the curve, avoid stagnation, and remain relevant over the long term. Moreover, innovation enhances resilience by diversifying revenue streams, expanding into new markets, and future-proofing against disruptive forces.

Customer-Centricity and Value Creation:

At the heart of successful innovation lies a deep understanding of customer needs and aspirations. By prioritizing customer-centricity, businesses can create value that resonates with their target audience, fostering loyalty and advocacy. Innovators anticipate emerging trends, anticipate future needs, and deliver solutions that exceed customer expectations, driving sustainable growth and profitability.

Cultivation of Organizational Culture and Talent:

Innovation flourishes in environments that foster creativity, collaboration, and experimentation. Businesses that cultivate a culture of innovation attract top talent, inspire employee engagement, and unleash the full potential of their workforce. By investing in innovation capabilities, training, and infrastructure, organizations can harness the collective ingenuity of their teams and drive transformative change from within.

Innovation is not a luxury reserved for a select few; it's a strategic imperative for businesses seeking to thrive in an increasingly competitive and uncertain world. By embracing innovation as a core value and integrating it into their DNA, entrepreneurs can unlock the key to long-term success and create a brighter future for themselves and their stakeholders.

- The Intersection of Creativity and Problem-Solving

At the heart of innovation lies the synergy between creativity and problem-solving. In this section, we explore how the dynamic interplay between these two elements fuels entrepreneurial success, driving the development of groundbreaking ideas and transformative solutions.

The Nature of Creativity:

Creativity is a complex and multifaceted phenomenon that encompasses a wide range of cognitive, emotional, and behavioral processes. It involves the generation of novel and valuable ideas, solutions, or insights that are both original and useful. While creativity is often associated with artistic endeavors, it is also integral to problem-solving, innovation, and entrepreneurship across diverse domains. Here, we comprehensively discuss the nature of creativity, exploring its multifaceted dimensions and debunking common myths:

1. **Cognitive Processes:**

a. **Divergent Thinking:** Creativity is characterized by divergent thinking, the ability to generate multiple ideas or solutions in response to a single problem or stimulus. Divergent thinking involves breaking free from conventional or linear thinking patterns and exploring alternative perspectives, possibilities, and associations.

b. **Associative Thinking**: Creativity often involves associative thinking, the ability to connect seemingly unrelated ideas, concepts, or experiences to generate new insights or solutions. Associative thinking relies on the brain's associative memory networks, which enable individuals to make novel connections and associations between disparate elements.

c. **Flexible Thinking**: Creativity requires flexible thinking, the ability to adapt and shift cognitive strategies, perspectives, and approaches in response to changing circumstances or constraints. Flexible thinkers are open-minded, adaptable, and willing to explore unconventional or unconventional paths to problem-solving and innovation.

2. Emotional Processes:

a. **Passion and Curiosity**: Creativity is fueled by passion and curiosity, the intrinsic motivation to explore, experiment, and create. Passionate individuals are driven by a deep sense of purpose or intrinsic interest in their creative pursuits, while curiosity motivates individuals to seek out new experiences, ideas, and challenges.

b. **Emotional Resilience**: Creativity often requires emotional resilience, the ability to persevere in the face of setbacks, failures, and criticism. Creative individuals are resilient in overcoming obstacles, managing self-doubt, and bouncing back from disappointments, enabling them to persist in their creative endeavors despite adversity.

3. Behavioral Processes:

a. **Experimentation and Risk-Taking:** Creativity involves experimentation and risk-taking, the willingness to explore new ideas, methods, and possibilities without fear of failure or judgment. Creative individuals are willing to take calculated risks, push boundaries, and challenge conventions in pursuit of innovative solutions.

b. **Collaboration and Feedback:** Creativity thrives in collaborative environments where individuals can exchange ideas, receive feedback, and build upon each other's contributions. Collaboration fosters creativity by providing diverse perspectives, insights, and expertise, while feedback helps refine and improve creative ideas through iterative processes of evaluation and refinement.

Debunking Common Myths:

1. **Myth:** Creativity is innate and cannot be learned.

   Reality: While some individuals may have a natural inclination towards creativity, creativity is a skill that can be developed and nurtured through practice, experimentation, and learning. Everyone has the potential to be creative with the right mindset and approach.

2. **Myth:** Creativity is limited to the arts.

Reality: Creativity is not limited to artistic pursuits; it is integral to problem-solving, innovation, and entrepreneurship across diverse domains, including science, technology, engineering, and business.

3. **Myth:** Creativity is a solitary endeavor.

Reality: While creativity often involves moments of solitary reflection and introspection, it also thrives in collaborative environments where individuals can exchange ideas, collaborate on projects, and build upon each other's contributions.

Creativity is a multifaceted phenomenon that involves cognitive, emotional, and behavioral processes. It encompasses divergent thinking, associative thinking, flexible thinking, passion, curiosity, emotional resilience, experimentation, risk-taking, collaboration, and feedback. By understanding the nature of creativity and debunking common myths, individuals can cultivate and unleash their creative potential to solve problems, innovate, and thrive in an increasingly complex and dynamic world.

The Art of Problem-Solving:

Effective problem-solving is a critical skill that is essential for success in both personal and professional contexts. It involves a systematic approach to identifying, analyzing, and resolving complex issues or challenges. Here, we comprehensively discuss the principles and methodologies of effective problem-solving, from defining the problem and gathering data to generating alternative solutions and evaluating outcomes:

1. Define the Problem:

a. **Identify the Root Cause**: Begin by clarifying the nature and scope of the problem, and identifying its underlying causes or contributing factors.

Understanding the root cause of the problem is essential for developing effective solutions.

b. **Establish Clear Objectives**: Define clear and specific objectives for solving the problem, outlining the desired outcomes and success criteria. Establishing clear objectives helps focus efforts and guide decision-making throughout the problem-solving process.

2. Gather Data and Information:

a. **Collect Relevant Data**: Gather relevant data and information related to the problem, using a variety of sources such as research studies, reports, surveys, and interviews. Collecting and analyzing data provides insights into the nature and scope of the problem, and helps inform decision-making.

b. **Analyze Data:** Analyze the collected data to identify patterns, trends, and correlations that may shed light on the underlying causes of the problem. Use data analysis techniques such as statistical analysis, trend analysis, and root cause analysis to extract meaningful insights.

3. Generate Alternative Solutions:

a. **Brainstorm Ideas:** Encourage brainstorming sessions to generate a wide range of potential solutions to the problem. Encourage creativity, open-mindedness, and divergent thinking to explore unconventional or innovative ideas.

b. **Evaluate Feasibility**: Evaluate the feasibility of each potential solution based on factors such as resources, time constraints, and potential risks. Consider the practicality, cost-effectiveness, and scalability of each solution before moving forward.

4. Evaluate and Select Solutions:

a. **Analyze Pros and Cons:** Assess the strengths and weaknesses of each potential solution, considering factors such as effectiveness, efficiency, and sustainability. Compare and contrast alternative solutions to determine their relative merits and drawbacks.

b. **Prioritize Solutions:** Prioritize potential solutions based on their alignment with established objectives, feasibility, and potential impact on achieving desired outcomes. Select the solution or combination of solutions that offer the best balance of benefits and risks.

5. Implement and Monitor:

a. **Develop an Action Plan:** Develop a detailed action plan outlining the steps, resources, and timelines required to implement the selected solution. Assign roles and responsibilities to team members, and establish clear communication channels to ensure accountability and coordination.

b. **Monitor Progress:** Monitor progress throughout the implementation process, tracking key performance indicators and milestones to gauge effectiveness and identify any issues or challenges that may arise. Make adjustments as needed to stay on course and address emerging concerns.

6. Evaluate Outcomes and Iterate:

a. **Measure Results:** Evaluate the outcomes of the problem-solving effort against established objectives and success criteria. Measure the impact of the solution on key performance metrics, and gather feedback from stakeholders to assess satisfaction and effectiveness.

b. **Learn from Experience:** Reflect on the problem-solving process and outcomes, identifying lessons learned and areas for improvement. Use insights gained from the experience to inform future problem-solving efforts and continuously refine and optimize strategies.

Effective problem-solving involves a systematic and structured approach that encompasses defining the problem, gathering data, generating alternative solutions, evaluating outcomes, and iterating based on feedback and experience. By following these principles and methodologies, individuals and teams can address complex challenges with confidence, creativity, and effectiveness, leading to successful outcomes and continuous improvement over time.

Creative Problem-Solving in Action:

Successful entrepreneurs excel at applying creative problem-solving techniques to navigate complex challenges and unlock new possibilities. Creative problem-solving is a critical skill that enables entrepreneurs to identify opportunities, overcome obstacles, and drive innovation in their ventures. Here, we comprehensively discuss how successful entrepreneurs apply creative problem-solving techniques:

1. **Embrace Ambiguity and Uncertainty:**

Successful entrepreneurs thrive in environments characterized by ambiguity and uncertainty, viewing challenges as opportunities for growth and learning. They are comfortable with taking calculated risks and embracing uncertainty, recognizing that it is often the path to innovation and discovery.

2. **Think Outside the Box:**

Successful entrepreneurs think outside the box, challenging conventional wisdom and exploring unconventional solutions to complex problems. They approach challenges with creativity, curiosity, and open-mindedness, seeking novel approaches that others may overlook.

3. Break Problems Down into Manageable Parts:

Complex challenges can often seem overwhelming, but successful entrepreneurs excel at breaking them down into manageable parts. They analyze problems systematically, identifying key components and breaking them down into smaller, more manageable tasks. This approach allows them to tackle complex issues one step at a time, making progress toward their goals.

4. Foster a Culture of Innovation:

Successful entrepreneurs foster a culture of innovation within their organizations, encouraging experimentation, collaboration, and risk-taking. They create environments where team members feel empowered to contribute ideas, challenge assumptions, and explore new possibilities. This culture of innovation fuels creativity and drives continuous improvement across the organization.

5. Adapt and Iterate:

Successful entrepreneurs understand that creative problem-solving is an iterative process that requires adaptability and flexibility. They are willing to pivot and adjust their strategies based on feedback and changing market conditions. This ability to adapt and iterate allows them to stay agile and responsive in the face of uncertainty and complexity.

6. Leverage Diverse Perspectives:

Successful entrepreneurs recognize the value of diverse perspectives in problem-solving and decision-making. They actively seek input from team members, advisors, customers, and other stakeholders with different backgrounds, experiences, and expertise. By leveraging diverse perspectives, entrepreneurs can generate a wide range of ideas and insights, leading to more creative and effective solutions.

7. Experiment and Test Hypotheses:

Successful entrepreneurs embrace experimentation as a core component of their problem-solving approach. They test hypotheses, conduct pilot studies, and gather feedback from real-world experiences to validate assumptions and refine their strategies. This iterative process of experimentation allows them to learn quickly, adapt their approach, and make informed decisions.

8. Stay Resilient and Persistent:

Creative problem-solving often involves facing setbacks, failures, and obstacles along the way. Successful entrepreneurs demonstrate resilience and persistence in the face of adversity, maintaining a positive attitude and persevering through challenges. They view failures as opportunities for learning and growth, using them to fuel their determination and drive for success.

Successful entrepreneurs apply creative problem-solving techniques to navigate complex challenges and unlock new possibilities in their ventures. By embracing ambiguity, thinking outside the box, breaking problems down into manageable parts, fostering a culture of innovation, adapting and iterating, leveraging diverse perspectives, experimenting and testing hypotheses, and staying resilient and persistent, entrepreneurs can overcome obstacles, seize opportunities, and achieve their goals. Creative problem-solving is a key driver of entrepreneurial success, enabling entrepreneurs to innovate, disrupt, and create value in an ever-changing and competitive business landscape.

The Role of Design Thinking:

Design thinking is a human-centered approach to innovation that focuses on understanding the needs, preferences, and behaviors of users to create products, services, and solutions that meet their needs effectively. It emphasizes empathy, iteration, and user-centricity as drivers of meaningful innovation. Here, we comprehensively discuss the principles of design thinking:

1. Empathy:

a. **Understanding User Needs:** Design thinking begins with empathy, the ability to understand and empathize with the needs, preferences, and experiences of users. Successful innovation requires a deep understanding of the people who will use the product or service, including their goals, challenges, and pain points.

b. **User Research and Observation**: Design thinkers engage in user research and observation to gain insights into user behavior, preferences, and motivations. They use techniques such as interviews, surveys, and ethnographic studies to gather qualitative and quantitative data, allowing them to develop a holistic understanding of user needs.

c. **Empathy Mapping**: Design thinkers create empathy maps to visualize and empathize with users' thoughts, feelings, and motivations. Empathy maps help identify key insights and opportunities for innovation by highlighting users' needs, desires, fears, and aspirations.

2. **Iteration**:

a. **Prototyping and Testing**: Design thinking emphasizes rapid prototyping and testing to iterate on ideas and solutions quickly. Design thinkers create low-fidelity prototypes, such as sketches, wireframes, or mockups, to visualize and communicate ideas. They gather feedback from users through usability testing and iterate on prototypes based on user feedback.

   b. **Fail Fast, Learn Quickly**: Design thinkers embrace a "fail fast, learn quickly" mindset, recognizing that failure is an inevitable part of the innovation process. They view failure as an opportunity for learning and improvement, using feedback from failed experiments to refine and iterate on their ideas.

   c. **Continuous Improvement**: Design thinking is an iterative process that involves continuous improvement based on feedback and experimentation. Design thinkers iterate on their ideas and solutions based on user feedback, market research, and evolving needs, continuously refining and optimizing their designs to better meet user needs and preferences.

3. User-Centricity:

a. **Design for Humans:** Design thinking is inherently user-centric, focusing on designing products, services, and experiences that are intuitive, enjoyable, and meaningful for users. Design thinkers prioritize human needs and experiences over technical or business constraints, ensuring that solutions are tailored to the needs and preferences of users.

b. **Co-Creation and Collaboration:** Design thinkers engage users as co-creators and collaborators in the design process, actively involving them in brainstorming, prototyping, and testing activities. They recognize the value of diverse perspectives and expertise, leveraging the collective intelligence of multidisciplinary teams to generate innovative solutions.

c. **User-Centered Evaluation:** Design thinkers evaluate the success of their solutions based on user-centered criteria, such as usability, satisfaction, and impact. They measure the effectiveness of their designs through user testing, feedback, and iterative refinement, ensuring that solutions meet user needs and deliver meaningful value.

Design thinking is a human-centered approach to innovation that emphasizes empathy, iteration, and user-centricity as drivers of meaningful innovation. By understanding user needs, iterating on ideas through rapid prototyping and testing, and prioritizing human-centered design principles, design thinkers can create products, services, and experiences that resonate with users and deliver lasting impact. Design thinking is a powerful framework for solving complex problems, driving innovation, and creating value in an increasingly user-centric and competitive business landscape.

Fostering Creativity and Problem-Solving Skills:

Fostering creativity and problem-solving skills within organizations and individuals is essential for driving innovation, adaptability, and success in today's dynamic and competitive business environment. Here, we comprehensively discuss practical strategies for fostering creativity and problem-solving skills:

1. Create a Culture of Innovation:

a. **Encourage Experimentation**: Create a culture that values experimentation, risk-taking, and learning from failure. Encourage employees to explore new ideas, take calculated risks, and experiment with different approaches to problem-solving.

b. **Promote Psychological Safety**: Foster an environment where employees feel safe to express their ideas, voice their opinions, and take risks without fear of judgment or reprisal. Promote open communication, constructive feedback, and a non-hierarchical approach to decision-making.

c. **Support Diversity and Inclusion**: Embrace diversity and inclusion as drivers of creativity and innovation. Create opportunities for collaboration and exchange of ideas among individuals from diverse backgrounds, perspectives, and experiences.

d. **Recognize and Reward Creativity**: Recognize and reward employees who demonstrate creativity, innovation, and problem-solving skills. Celebrate successes, acknowledge contributions, and provide incentives for creative thinking and initiative.

2. **Provide Training and Development Opportunities:**

a. **Offer Training Programs**: Provide training programs and workshops focused on creativity, innovation, and problem-solving skills. Offer courses on design thinking, creative problem-solving, brainstorming techniques, and other relevant topics to help employees develop their creative capabilities.

b. **Support Continuous Learning**: Encourage employees to pursue continuous learning and professional development opportunities. Provide access to resources such as books, online courses, and seminars to help employees enhance their creative and problem-solving skills.

c. Facilitate Cross-Functional Collaboration:

Facilitate cross-functional collaboration and knowledge sharing among teams and departments. Encourage employees to collaborate on projects outside their areas of expertise, fostering interdisciplinary approaches to problem-solving and innovation.

3. Foster a Supportive Work Environment:

a. **Provide Resources and Tools:** Ensure that employees have access to the resources, tools, and technologies they need to support their creative endeavors. Provide access to creative software, prototyping tools, and collaborative platforms to facilitate idea generation and experimentation.

b. **Create Flexible Workspaces**: Create flexible workspaces that support collaboration, creativity, and innovation. Design office environments that foster creativity and interaction, with spaces for brainstorming, ideation, and informal meetings.

c. **Encourage Work-Life Balance**: Promote work-life balance and well-being initiatives that support employee creativity and productivity. Encourage employees to take breaks, recharge, and pursue hobbies and interests outside of work, fostering a healthy and balanced lifestyle conducive to creative thinking.

4. Promote Mindfulness and Creative Practices:

a. **Encourage Mindfulness:** Promote mindfulness practices such as meditation, yoga, and deep breathing exercises to help employees reduce stress, enhance focus, and stimulate creative thinking. Offer mindfulness workshops or classes to support employee well-being and creativity.

b. **Foster Creative Habits**: Encourage employees to cultivate creative habits and routines that support their creative process. Encourage practices such as journaling, sketching, and idea-generation exercises to stimulate creativity and generate new insights.

c. **Provide Time for Reflection:** Create opportunities for employees to reflect on their work, ideas, and experiences. Encourage employees to set aside time for reflection and introspection, allowing them to gain new perspectives, insights, and inspiration.

5. Lead by Example:

a. **Lead by Example**: Demonstrate a commitment to creativity and problem-solving by leading by example. Encourage open-mindedness, curiosity, and a willingness to challenge the status quo. Model creative thinking and behavior in your approach to problem-solving and decision-making.

b. **Support Employee Initiatives**: Support and empower employees to pursue their creative ideas and initiatives. Provide resources, guidance, and mentorship to help employees develop and implement their creative projects and innovations.

c. **Foster a Growth Mindset**: Cultivate a growth mindset that embraces challenges, sees failure as an opportunity for learning, and values effort and perseverance. Encourage employees to adopt a growth mindset and embrace challenges as opportunities for growth and development.

Fostering creativity and problem-solving skills within organizations and individuals requires a multifaceted approach that involves creating a culture of innovation, providing training and development opportunities, fostering a supportive work environment, promoting mindfulness and creative practices, and leading by example. By implementing these practical strategies, organizations can cultivate a workforce that is empowered, inspired, and equipped to tackle complex challenges, drive innovation, and achieve success in today's fast-paced and ever-changing business landscape.

The intersection of creativity and problem-solving is where ideas take flight, challenges become opportunities, and innovation thrives. By embracing the creative potential within themselves and their teams, entrepreneurs can unlock new horizons of possibility and chart a course towards sustainable success in the ever-evolving landscape of entrepreneurship.

CHAPTER 2: UNLEASHING CREATIVE POTENTIAL

Welcome to the exhilarating journey of unlocking creative potential in the pursuit of entrepreneurial success. In this chapter, aptly titled "Unleashing Creative Potential," we embark on a voyage into the boundless realms of imagination, where innovation begins with the daring exploration of new ideas and the relentless pursuit of unconventional solutions.

Creativity is the lifeblood of entrepreneurship, fueling the ingenuity and resilience needed to navigate the complex challenges of today's business landscape. Yet, for many aspiring entrepreneurs, unlocking their creative potential can feel like a daunting task, hindered by self-doubt, fear of failure, and a lack of clarity on where to begin.

Fear not, for this chapter serves as your compass, guiding you through the labyrinth of creativity and equipping you with the tools, techniques, and mindset needed to unleash your creative potential in pursuit of entrepreneurial greatness.

We'll delve into the essence of creativity, demystifying its elusive nature and unveiling the cognitive processes that drive innovative thinking. From cultivating curiosity and embracing uncertainty to fostering a culture of experimentation and embracing failure as a stepping stone to success, we'll explore the principles that underpin creative genius and empower you to tap into your innate capacity for innovation.

Moreover, we'll delve into practical strategies for overcoming common creativity blocks and nurturing a creative mindset that thrives in the face of adversity. Through inspiring anecdotes, hands-on exercises, and thought-provoking insights, you'll discover how to break free from the constraints of conventional thinking, transcend boundaries, and unlock the full spectrum of your creative potential.

So, prepare to embark on a transformative journey of self-discovery and creative exploration. As we peel back the layers of inhibition and unleash the creative forces within, you'll emerge emboldened, inspired, and ready to embark on a path of entrepreneurial innovation that knows no bounds.

- Cultivating an Entrepreneurial Mindset

At the core of every successful entrepreneur lies an entrepreneurial mindset—a unique set of attitudes, beliefs, and habits that drive visionary thinking, resilience, and a bias towards action. In this section, we explore the process of cultivating an entrepreneurial mindset, unpacking the key principles and practices that empower individuals to think and act like entrepreneurs.

1. **Embracing Opportunity and Risk:**

Entrepreneurial mindset begins with a fundamental shift in perception—an openness to seeing challenges as opportunities and risks as potential rewards. Entrepreneurs learn to embrace uncertainty, viewing setbacks as valuable learning experiences and reframing failures as stepping stones to success. By cultivating a growth mindset and adopting a positive attitude towards risk-taking, individuals can overcome fear and inertia, unleashing their potential to innovate and create value.

2. Fostering Resilience and Adaptability:

In the fast-paced world of entrepreneurship, resilience is essential for weathering storms and bouncing back from setbacks. Entrepreneurs cultivate resilience by developing coping strategies, building a strong support network, and maintaining a sense of perspective amidst adversity. Moreover, they embrace adaptability, recognizing the need to pivot, iterate, and evolve in response to changing circumstances. By remaining agile and resilient in the face of uncertainty, entrepreneurs can navigate challenges with confidence and emerge stronger on the other side.

3. Nurturing Curiosity and Creativity:

Entrepreneurial mindset thrives on curiosity—an insatiable hunger for knowledge, exploration, and discovery. Entrepreneurs cultivate curiosity by asking probing questions, seeking out new experiences, and challenging assumptions. Moreover, they harness the power of creativity to generate innovative solutions and envision possibilities beyond the status quo. By nurturing a curious and creative mindset, individuals can unlock new opportunities, spark inspiration, and drive transformative change in their lives and communities.

4. Adopting a Customer-Centric Focus:

Successful entrepreneurs understand the importance of putting the customer at the center of their business. They cultivate empathy, seeking to understand customer needs, desires, and pain points. By adopting a customer-centric mindset, entrepreneurs can identify unmet needs, anticipate market trends, and design solutions that resonate with their target audience. Moreover, they prioritize continuous feedback and iteration, using customer insights to refine their products, services, and business models over time.

5. **Taking Action and Building Momentum:**

The entrepreneurial mindset is characterized by a bias towards action—a willingness to take calculated risks and pursue bold ideas with conviction. Entrepreneurs understand that ideas alone are not enough; execution is key to success. They break down complex goals into actionable steps, set ambitious yet achievable targets, and cultivate a sense of urgency to drive progress. By consistently taking action and building momentum, entrepreneurs can turn their visions into reality and create lasting impact in the world.

Cultivating an entrepreneurial mindset is a transformative journey—an ongoing process of self-discovery, growth, and evolution. By embracing opportunity, fostering resilience, nurturing curiosity, adopting a customer-centric focus, and taking decisive action, individuals can unlock their entrepreneurial potential and embark on a path of innovation, creativity, and fulfilment.

- Techniques for Generating Innovative Ideas

Innovation is fueled by a continuous flow of fresh ideas that challenge the status quo and push the boundaries of possibility. In this section, we explore a variety of techniques and methodologies for generating innovative ideas, empowering individuals to tap into their creative potential and unleashing groundbreaking solutions to complex problems.

1. Brainstorming:

Brainstorming is a classic technique for generating a wide range of ideas in a collaborative setting. Participants are encouraged to suspend judgment and freely share their thoughts, no matter how wild or unconventional. By leveraging the diversity of perspectives and building upon each other's ideas, brainstorming sessions can spark creativity and uncover novel solutions to challenges.

2. Mind Mapping:

Mind mapping is a visual technique for organizing thoughts and exploring connections between ideas. Starting with a central concept or problem statement, individuals branch out to create a network of related concepts, themes, and potential solutions. Mind maps can serve as powerful tools for brainstorming, problem-solving, and generating innovative insights by visualizing the relationships between different elements of a problem or opportunity.

3. Design Thinking:

Design thinking is a human-centered approach to innovation that prioritizes empathy, experimentation, and iteration. It involves a structured process of empathizing with users, defining their needs and pain points, ideating potential solutions, prototyping concepts, and gathering feedback to refine and improve upon them. Design thinking encourages a bias towards action and fosters a collaborative mindset, empowering individuals to co-create innovative solutions that address real-world challenges.

4. SCAMPER Technique:

The SCAMPER technique is a creative thinking tool that prompts individuals to explore different dimensions of an existing idea or concept by asking a series of questions: Substitute, Combine, Adapt, Modify, Put to Another Use, Eliminate, and Reverse. By systematically applying these prompts to an idea, individuals can generate a multitude of variations and enhancements, leading to innovative breakthroughs and fresh perspectives.

5. Random Stimulus:

Random stimulus techniques involve introducing unexpected elements or constraints to spur creative thinking and disrupt conventional thought patterns. This could involve using random words, images, or objects as prompts for ideation, forcing individuals to make novel associations and connections. By embracing randomness and serendipity, individuals can unlock new perspectives and uncover hidden opportunities for innovation.

6. Analogous Inspiration:

Analogous inspiration involves drawing inspiration from unrelated domains or industries to generate innovative ideas. By exploring how similar challenges have been addressed in different contexts, individuals can gain fresh insights and apply creative solutions to their problems. Analogous inspiration encourages lateral thinking and cross-pollination of ideas, fostering a culture of innovation that transcends traditional boundaries and disciplines.

Generating innovative ideas is a multifaceted process that requires a blend of creativity, curiosity, and structured thinking. By leveraging a diverse range of techniques—from brainstorming and mind mapping to design thinking and random stimulus—

individuals can unlock their creative potential and unleash a torrent of fresh ideas that drive meaningful change and propel innovation forward.

- Overcoming Common Creativity Blocks

Creativity blocks are barriers that hinder the flow of innovative ideas, stifling entrepreneurial potential and impeding progress. In this section, we explore the common creativity blocks that entrepreneurs encounter and provide strategies for overcoming them, empowering individuals to unleash their creative potential and drive meaningful innovation.

1. Fear of Failure:

Fear of failure is one of the most pervasive creativity blocks, paralyzing individuals and preventing them from taking risks or pursuing ambitious ideas. To overcome this block, entrepreneurs must reframe failure as a natural part of the creative process—a valuable opportunity for learning and growth. By embracing failure as a stepping stone to success and cultivating a growth mindset, individuals can overcome their fears and pursue innovative solutions with confidence.

2. Perfectionism:

Perfectionism is another common creativity block that can stifle creativity and hinder progress. Entrepreneurs often feel pressure to produce flawless solutions, leading to procrastination, self-doubt, and a reluctance to experiment. To overcome perfectionism, individuals must embrace imperfection and adopt an iterative approach to innovation. By embracing experimentation, iteration, and feedback, entrepreneurs can break free from the shackles of perfectionism and unleash their creative potential.

3. Lack of Inspiration:

A lack of inspiration can leave entrepreneurs feeling stuck in a rut, struggling to generate fresh ideas or solve challenging problems. To overcome this block, individuals must actively seek out sources of inspiration and expose themselves to new experiences, perspectives, and stimuli. Whether through travel, art, literature, or conversations with diverse individuals, entrepreneurs can reignite their creative spark and uncover new opportunities for innovation.

4. Over thinking:

Over thinking is a creativity block that can lead to analysis paralysis, preventing entrepreneurs from taking action or making decisions. To overcome this block, individuals must learn to quiet their inner critic and trust their intuition. By adopting a bias towards action and embracing experimentation, entrepreneurs can break free from the cycle of over thinking and unleash their creative potential.

5. Lack of Constraints:

Paradoxically, a lack of constraints can also hinder creativity by leaving individuals feeling overwhelmed or directionless. To overcome this block, entrepreneurs can introduce artificial constraints or challenges to focus their creativity and stimulate innovation. Whether through time limits, budget constraints, or design challenges, constraints can provide the structure and direction needed to channel creative energy towards meaningful solutions.

6. Negative Environment:

A negative environment—whether it's toxic colleagues, unsupportive stakeholders, or a lack of resources—can dampen creativity and demotivate entrepreneurs. To overcome this block, individuals must surround themselves with supportive peers, mentors, and collaborators who nurture their creative spirit and provide encouragement. By creating a positive and empowering environment, entrepreneurs can overcome obstacles, stay motivated, and unlock their full creative potential.

Creativity blocks are inevitable obstacles on the path to entrepreneurial success, but they need not be insurmountable. By recognizing common creativity blocks and employing strategies to overcome them—whether through reframing failure, embracing imperfection, seeking inspiration, taking action, introducing constraints, or fostering a positive environment—entrepreneurs can unleash their creative potential and drive meaningful innovation that propels their ventures forward.

CHAPTER 3: NAVIGATING MARKET DISRUPTION

Welcome to the dynamic landscape of market disruption—an era characterized by rapid technological advancements, shifting consumer behaviors, and unprecedented levels of uncertainty. In this chapter, aptly titled "Navigating Market Disruption," we embark on a journey to explore the forces reshaping industries and challenging traditional business models, empowering entrepreneurs to thrive amidst change and uncertainty.

Market disruption is not a new phenomenon, but its pace and scale have accelerated in recent years, driven by innovations in digital technology, globalization, and changing societal values. Disruptive startups and agile incumbents alike are challenging established norms, reshuffling competitive landscapes, and revolutionizing entire industries.

In this chapter, we delve into the essence of market disruption, dissecting its causes, manifestations, and implications for entrepreneurs. We explore the strategies and tactics that enable businesses to not only survive but also thrive in disruptive environments, seizing opportunities and leveraging change as a catalyst for growth.

From identifying disruptive trends and understanding their impact on traditional business models to embracing agility and innovation as survival imperatives, we equip entrepreneurs with the tools, insights, and mindset needed to navigate market disruption with confidence and resilience.

Moreover, we draw inspiration from real-world examples and case studies of companies that have successfully navigated market disruption, distilling actionable lessons and best practices that entrepreneurs can apply to their ventures.

As we embark on this transformative journey together, prepare to challenge assumptions, embrace uncertainty, and harness the power of disruption to propel your entrepreneurial endeavors to new heights. The road ahead may be fraught with challenges, but with the right strategies and mindset, market disruption can be a source of opportunity and growth for those bold enough to seize it.

- Identifying and Analyzing Disruptive Trends

In today's rapidly evolving business landscape, staying ahead of the curve requires a keen awareness of disruptive trends that have the potential to reshape industries and redefine competitive dynamics. In this section, we explore the process of identifying and analyzing disruptive trends, equipping entrepreneurs with the foresight and strategic insight needed to navigate market disruption and seize growth opportunities.

1. Environmental Scanning:

Environmental scanning involves systematically gathering and analyzing information from various sources to identify emerging trends, market shifts, and disruptive forces. Entrepreneurs can monitor industry publications, market research reports, social media channels, and technology forums to stay abreast of developments and spot early indicators of disruption. By conducting regular scans of the external environment, entrepreneurs can proactively identify potential threats and opportunities for innovation.

2. Industry Analysis:

Industry analysis involves assessing the competitive landscape, market dynamics, and key drivers of change within a specific industry or sector. Entrepreneurs can use tools such as Porter's Five Forces framework to analyze the intensity of competition, the threat of new entrants, the power of buyers and suppliers, and the availability of substitutes. By understanding the underlying forces shaping industry dynamics, entrepreneurs can identify potential disruptors and anticipate shifts in market trends.

3. Technology Trends:

Technology trends play a significant role in driving market disruption, enabling new business models, and transforming consumer behavior. Entrepreneurs can track emerging technologies such as artificial intelligence, blockchain, Internet of Things (IoT), and augmented reality to identify potential disruptors and opportunities for innovation. By understanding the implications of technology trends on their industry and business model, entrepreneurs can proactively adapt and capitalize on emerging opportunities.

4. Consumer Insights:

Consumer behavior is another key driver of market disruption, as changing preferences, attitudes, and expectations shape demand patterns and market dynamics. Entrepreneurs can leverage data analytics, market research, and customer feedback to gain insights into evolving consumer needs and preferences. By understanding the motivations and pain points of their target audience, entrepreneurs can identify unmet needs and develop innovative solutions that resonate with consumers.

5. Macro-Economic Trends:

Macroeconomic trends, such as demographic shifts, geopolitical developments, and regulatory changes, can also influence market dynamics and drive disruption. Entrepreneurs can monitor macroeconomic indicators, such as GDP growth, inflation rates, and unemployment levels, to identify potential opportunities and threats. By understanding the broader economic context in which their business operates, entrepreneurs can anticipate changes in consumer behavior, industry regulations, and competitive dynamics.

Identifying and analyzing disruptive trends is a critical process for entrepreneurs seeking to stay ahead of the curve and capitalize on emerging opportunities. By conducting environmental scans, industry analyses, tracking technology trends, gaining consumer insights, and monitoring macroeconomic indicators, entrepreneurs can develop a comprehensive understanding of the forces shaping their industry and business environment. Armed with strategic insight and foresight, entrepreneurs can proactively adapt to market disruption, innovate new solutions, and position their ventures for long-term success in a rapidly changing world.

- Strategies for Responding to Market Disruption

Market disruption poses both challenges and opportunities for businesses, requiring strategic agility and innovation to thrive amidst change. In this section, we explore a range of strategies that entrepreneurs can employ to respond effectively to market disruption, leveraging change as a catalyst for growth and differentiation.

1. Embrace Innovation:

Innovation lies at the heart of responding to market disruption. Entrepreneurs must foster a culture of innovation within their organizations, encouraging creativity, experimentation, and a willingness to challenge the status quo. By investing in research and development, embracing emerging technologies, and continuously iterating on their products and services, businesses can stay ahead of the curve and remain competitive in disruptive markets.

2. Pivot and Adapt:

Market disruption often necessitates a strategic pivot or adaptation to evolving market conditions. Entrepreneurs must be willing to reassess their business models, value propositions, and go-to-market strategies in response to changing customer needs and competitive pressures. By remaining agile and adaptable, businesses can capitalize on new opportunities and mitigate the risks posed by disruptive forces.

3. Focus on Customer Experience:

In disruptive markets, customer experience becomes a key differentiator for businesses seeking to stand out amidst competition. Entrepreneurs must prioritize understanding and meeting the evolving needs and preferences of their customers, delivering exceptional experiences at every touch point. By investing in customer relationship management, personalization, and service excellence, businesses can build loyalty, drive repeat business, and attract new customers in disruptive markets.

4. Collaborate and Partner:

Collaboration and partnership can be powerful strategies for responding to market disruption. Entrepreneurs can form strategic alliances with complementary businesses, startups, or industry incumbents to leverage their expertise, resources, and market presence. By pooling resources, sharing risks, and co-creating innovative solutions, businesses can accelerate their response to disruption and create value for customers and stakeholders.

5. Invest in Talent and Capabilities:

Responding to market disruption requires a skilled and adaptable workforce capable of navigating change and driving innovation. Entrepreneurs must invest in talent development, training, and recruitment to build a team capable of responding effectively to disruptive forces. By fostering a culture of continuous learning, empowerment, and collaboration, businesses can harness the full potential of their employees and position themselves for success in dynamic markets.

6. Diversify Revenue Streams:

Diversification can be a valuable strategy for mitigating the risks posed by market disruption. Entrepreneurs can explore new markets, product lines, or revenue streams to reduce reliance on a single source of income and spread risk across different business areas. By diversifying their offerings and revenue streams, businesses can adapt to changing market conditions, capitalize on emerging opportunities, and maintain resilience in the face of disruption.

7. Anticipate Future Trends:

A successful response to market disruption requires a forward-thinking approach that anticipates future trends and positions businesses for success in the long term. Entrepreneurs must stay abreast of emerging technologies, consumer trends, and industry developments to proactively identify opportunities and threats. By investing in market research, trend analysis, and scenario planning, businesses can develop the strategic foresight and agility needed to navigate disruption and thrive in dynamic markets.

Market disruption is inevitable in today's fast-paced business environment, but it need not be a source of fear or uncertainty. By embracing innovation, pivoting and adapting, focusing on customer experience, collaborating and partnering, investing in talent and capabilities, diversifying revenue streams, and anticipating future trends, entrepreneurs can respond effectively to market disruption and position their businesses for long-term success in a constantly evolving landscape.

- Case Studies of Successful Disruption and Adaptation

In the dynamic landscape of entrepreneurship, success often hinges on the ability to disrupt existing markets and adapt to changing conditions. In this section, we examine case studies of businesses that have successfully navigated market disruption, demonstrating resilience, innovation, and strategic agility in the face of adversity.

1. **Netflix:**

Netflix is a quintessential example of a company that disrupted the traditional video rental industry and adapted to the rise of digital streaming. By recognizing the shifting preferences of consumers towards on-demand content and the convenience of streaming, Netflix transitioned from a DVD rental service to a digital streaming platform. Through strategic investments in content production, personalized recommendations, and global expansion, Netflix has become a dominant player in the entertainment industry, reshaping how audiences consume media worldwide.

2. Amazon:

Amazon is another example of disruptive innovation and adaptation. Originally an online bookstore, Amazon has evolved into a retail behemoth that revolutionized e-commerce and cloud computing. By prioritizing customer-centricity, continuous experimentation, and technological innovation, Amazon has expanded its product offerings, disrupted traditional retail models, and transformed entire industries. Through acquisitions, investments in logistics and infrastructure, and the launch of innovative services such as Amazon Prime, Amazon continues to set the bar for disruption and adaptation in the digital age.

3. Tesla:

Tesla has disrupted the automotive industry by pioneering electric vehicles and renewable energy solutions. By challenging the status quo of the automotive industry, Tesla has redefined consumer expectations for performance, sustainability, and innovation. Through a relentless focus on innovation, vertical integration, and market disruption, Tesla has become a leader in electric vehicles, energy storage, and solar power. Despite facing challenges and sceptics, Tesla has demonstrated resilience and adaptability, continuously pushing the boundaries of innovation and sustainability in transportation and energy.

4. Airbnb:

Airbnb disrupted the hospitality industry by democratizing accommodations and empowering homeowners to monetize their properties. By leveraging technology and the sharing economy,

Airbnb created a platform that connects travelers with unique lodging experiences worldwide. Through community building, user-generated content, and personalized recommendations, Airbnb has disrupted traditional hotel chains and transformed how people travel and experience new destinations. Despite regulatory challenges and criticism, Airbnb has adapted its business model, expanded into new markets, and diversified its offerings to sustain growth and maintain its position as a disruptor in the travel industry.

5. Spotify:

Spotify disrupted the music industry by offering a convenient and affordable alternative to traditional music consumption. By providing access to a vast library of songs on-demand, Spotify revolutionized how people discover, stream, and share music. Through personalized playlists, algorithmic recommendations, and social sharing features, Spotify has created a platform that caters to diverse musical tastes and preferences. Despite facing resistance from record labels and artists, Spotify has adapted its business model, forged partnerships, and expanded its user base globally, solidifying its position as a leader in the music streaming industry. These case studies illustrate the power of disruption and adaptation in driving entrepreneurial success. By challenging conventional wisdom, embracing innovation, and adapting to changing market conditions, these businesses have not only survived but thrived amidst disruption. Their stories serve as valuable lessons for entrepreneurs seeking to navigate uncertainty, seize opportunities, and create lasting impact in a rapidly evolving business landscape.

CHAPTER 4: BUILDING A CULTURE OF INNOVATION

Welcome to the transformative journey of building a culture of innovation—a journey that empowers organizations to unleash the full creative potential of their teams, drive meaningful change, and stay ahead of the curve in an increasingly competitive landscape. In this chapter, aptly titled "Building a Culture of Innovation," we explore the essential principles, strategies, and practices that underpin a thriving culture of innovation within organizations.

Innovation is not merely about generating groundbreaking ideas; it's about creating an environment where creativity, experimentation, and collaboration flourish. A culture of innovation fosters a mindset of continuous learning, adaptation, and growth, empowering individuals at all levels to challenge the status quo, embrace uncertainty, and push the boundaries of what's possible.

In this chapter, we delve into the foundational elements of building a culture of innovation, from leadership commitment and organizational values to employee empowerment and infrastructure support. We examine how successful organizations cultivate a climate that encourages risk-taking, celebrates failure as a learning opportunity, and rewards creativity and initiative.

Moreover, we explore practical strategies and best practices for fostering a culture of innovation, drawing insights from real-world examples and case studies of organizations that have successfully embedded innovation into their DNA. From Google's "20% time" policy to 3M's "15% rule," we uncover the tactics and approaches that have enabled companies to harness the collective intelligence of their workforce and drive transformative change.

As we embark on this journey together, prepare to challenge assumptions, embrace diversity of thought, and cultivate an environment where every voice is heard, and every idea is valued. By building a culture of innovation, organizations can unlock new opportunities, drive sustainable growth, and create a lasting impact that transcends boundaries and transforms industries.

- Fostering a Culture that Encourages Experimentation and Risk-Taking

Innovation thrives in environments where experimentation and risk-taking are not only accepted but encouraged. In this section, we delve into the process of fostering a culture that embraces experimentation and risk-taking, empowering individuals to explore new ideas, challenge the status quo, and drive meaningful change within organizations.

1. Leadership Commitment:

Fostering a culture of experimentation and risk-taking starts with leadership commitment. Leaders must communicate a clear vision for innovation, articulate the importance of experimentation in achieving strategic objectives, and lead by example by taking calculated risks themselves. By demonstrating a willingness to embrace uncertainty and learn from failure, leaders set the tone for a culture that values experimentation and rewards initiative.

2. Psychological Safety:

Psychological safety is essential for fostering a culture where individuals feel empowered to take risks and share new ideas without fear of judgment or reprisal. Leaders must create an environment where employees feel safe to express dissenting opinions, challenge assumptions, and experiment with new approaches. By fostering trust, openness, and respect, organizations can cultivate a culture of psychological safety that encourages innovation and fosters creativity.

3. Encourage Curiosity and Learning:

Curiosity is the fuel that drives experimentation and innovation. Organizations must encourage a culture of continuous learning, curiosity, and inquiry, where employees are encouraged to ask questions, seek out new knowledge, and explore diverse perspectives. By providing opportunities for skill development, cross-functional collaboration, and exposure to new ideas, organizations can empower employees to experiment and take risks in pursuit of innovative solutions.

4. Celebrate Failure as a Learning Opportunity:

Failure is an inevitable part of the experimentation process and should be celebrated as a learning opportunity rather than stigmatized. Organizations must shift their mindset towards failure, reframing it as a natural part of the innovation journey and an opportunity for growth and learning. By destigmatizing failure, organizations can create a culture where employees feel empowered to take risks, learn from mistakes, and iterate on their ideas to achieve success.

5. Provide Resources and Support:

Experimentation requires resources, support, and infrastructure to thrive. Organizations must provide employees with the tools, time, and autonomy needed to explore new ideas and pursue innovative projects. By investing in innovation labs, incubators, and cross-functional teams, organizations can create a supportive ecosystem that encourages experimentation and provides a safe space for testing new concepts and prototypes.

6. Recognize and Reward Innovation:

Recognizing and rewarding innovation is essential for reinforcing a culture that values experimentation and risk-taking. Organizations must celebrate successes, acknowledge individuals who take calculated risks and reward innovative thinking and initiative. By incorporating innovation metrics into performance evaluations, incentive structures, and recognition programs, organizations can align employee behaviors with the values of experimentation and risk-taking.

Fostering a culture that encourages experimentation and risk-taking is essential for driving innovation and staying competitive in today's rapidly changing business environment. By cultivating leadership commitment, psychological safety, curiosity, learning, celebrating failure, providing resources and support, and recognizing and rewarding innovation, organizations can create an environment where experimentation thrives, and employees are empowered to unleash their creative potential and drive meaningful change.

- Implementing Effective Innovation Processes

Innovation is not a haphazard endeavor; it requires a systematic approach and well-defined processes to channel creative energy into tangible outcomes. In this section, we delve into the process of implementing effective innovation processes, empowering organizations to systematically generate, evaluate, and implement innovative ideas that drive growth and competitive advantage.

1. Establish Clear Objectives:

Effective innovation processes begin with clear objectives aligned with organizational goals and strategic priorities. Organizations must define what they seek to achieve through innovation—whether it's enhancing products and services, improving operational efficiency, entering new markets, or fostering a culture of continuous improvement. By articulating clear objectives, organizations can focus their innovation efforts and allocate resources effectively.

2. Foster a Culture of Innovation:

A culture of innovation is essential for nurturing creativity, collaboration, and experimentation within organizations. Leaders must cultivate an environment where employees feel empowered to challenge the status quo, share new ideas, and take calculated risks. By fostering psychological safety, celebrating diversity of thought, and providing opportunities for learning and development, organizations can create a culture where innovation thrives.

3. Ideation and Brainstorming:

Ideation and brainstorming sessions are critical for generating a wide range of innovative ideas within organizations. Organizations can host structured brainstorming sessions, hackathons, or innovation challenges to solicit ideas from employees across different departments and levels. By providing a platform for ideation and encouraging diverse perspectives, organizations can tap into the collective intelligence of their workforce and uncover novel solutions to complex challenges.

4. Evaluation and Prioritization:

Once ideas have been generated, they must be systematically evaluated and prioritized based on their alignment with organizational objectives, feasibility, potential impact, and resource requirements. Organizations can use frameworks such as SWOT analysis, cost-benefit analysis, or scoring models to evaluate and prioritize ideas objectively. By involving cross-functional teams in the evaluation process, organizations can leverage diverse expertise and perspectives to make informed decisions about which ideas to pursue.

5. Prototyping and Experimentation:

Prototyping and experimentation are essential for testing and refining innovative ideas before full-scale implementation. Organizations can create prototypes, minimum viable products (MVPs), or pilot projects to validate assumptions, gather feedback from stakeholders, and iterate on concepts rapidly. By adopting a lean approach to prototyping and experimentation, organizations can minimize risk, optimize resource allocation, and accelerate the innovation process.

6. Implementation and Scaling:

Once ideas have been validated through prototyping and experimentation, they can be implemented and scaled across the organization. Organizations must develop implementation plans, allocate resources, and establish accountability mechanisms to ensure successful execution. By providing training, support, and incentives for adoption, organizations can drive cultural change and embed innovative practices into their day-to-day operations.

7. Continuous Improvement and Learning:

Innovation is an iterative process that requires continuous improvement and learning. Organizations must establish mechanisms for gathering feedback, monitoring outcomes, and iterating on solutions based on real-world results. By fostering a culture of reflection, adaptation, and continuous improvement, organizations can continuously evolve and stay ahead of the curve in an ever-changing business environment.

Implementing effective innovation processes is essential for driving sustainable growth and maintaining competitiveness in today's rapidly evolving business landscape. By establishing clear objectives, fostering a culture of innovation, facilitating ideation and brainstorming, evaluating and prioritizing ideas, prototyping and experimentation, implementing and scaling solutions, and embracing continuous improvement and learning, organizations can systematically harness the power of innovation to achieve their strategic objectives and create lasting value for stakeholders.

- Encouraging Collaboration and Diversity of Thought

Innovation thrives in environments where collaboration and diversity of thought are embraced. In this section, we explore the process of encouraging collaboration and diversity of thought within organizations, empowering teams to leverage their collective intelligence, perspectives, and experiences to drive innovation and problem-solving.

1. Create a Culture of Psychological Safety:

Psychological safety is essential for fostering open communication, trust, and collaboration within teams. Leaders must create an environment where employees feel empowered to express their opinions, share ideas, and challenge assumptions without fear of judgment or reprisal. By promoting respect, empathy, and inclusivity, organizations can create a culture of psychological safety where diverse voices are valued and heard.

2. Build Cross-Functional Teams:

Cross-functional teams bring together individuals with diverse backgrounds, expertise, and perspectives to tackle complex problems and drive innovation. Organizations can assemble multidisciplinary teams comprising members from different departments, levels of seniority, and areas of expertise to bring fresh insights and approaches to the table. By breaking down silos and promoting collaboration across functional boundaries, organizations can foster creativity and drive holistic solutions.

3. Facilitate Open Communication and Knowledge Sharing:

Effective collaboration relies on open communication and knowledge sharing among team members. Organizations must provide platforms and channels for employees to exchange ideas, insights, and best practices freely. Whether through team meetings, brainstorming sessions, collaborative tools, or knowledge-sharing platforms, organizations can facilitate communication and foster a culture of transparency and collaboration.

4. Encourage Constructive Conflict:

Constructive conflict can spark creativity, challenge assumptions, and lead to better decision-making within teams. Organizations must encourage healthy debate, dissent, and disagreement among team members while maintaining respect and civility. By embracing diverse viewpoints and encouraging critical thinking, organizations can avoid groupthink and surface innovative solutions to complex problems.

5. Foster Inclusive Leadership:

Inclusive leadership is essential for fostering collaboration and diversity of thought within teams. Leaders must actively seek out diverse perspectives, encourage participation from all team members, and create opportunities for underrepresented voices to be heard. By fostering a sense of belonging and inclusion, leaders can unleash the full potential of their teams and drive innovation through diverse viewpoints and experiences.

6. Embrace Diversity and Inclusion:

Diversity and inclusion are essential for driving innovation and creativity within organizations. Organizations must actively recruit, retain, and promote individuals from diverse backgrounds, experiences, and perspectives. By embracing diversity in gender, race, ethnicity, age, sexual orientation, and cognitive style, organizations can foster a culture of creativity, innovation, and resilience that reflects the diversity of their employees and customers.

7. Provide Training and Development:

Training and development programs can help employees develop the skills and mindset needed to collaborate effectively and embrace diversity of thought. Organizations can offer workshops, seminars, and coaching sessions on topics such as communication, conflict resolution, cultural competence, and unconscious bias. By investing in employee development, organizations can equip their teams with the tools and techniques needed to navigate diverse perspectives and collaborate successfully.

Encouraging collaboration and diversity of thought is essential for driving innovation, creativity, and problem-solving within organizations. By creating a culture of psychological safety, building cross-functional teams, facilitating open communication, encouraging constructive conflict, fostering inclusive leadership, embracing diversity and inclusion, and providing training and development, organizations can unleash the full potential of their teams and harness the power of collaboration to achieve their strategic objectives and drive sustainable growth.

CHAPTER 5:

HARNESSING TECHNOLOGY FOR ENTREPRENEURIAL SUCCESS

Welcome to the exciting world of harnessing technology for entrepreneurial success—an era where innovative technologies are revolutionizing industries, empowering entrepreneurs to disrupt traditional business models, and creating new opportunities for growth and innovation. In this chapter, aptly titled "Harnessing Technology for Entrepreneurial Success," we explore the transformative potential of technology in driving entrepreneurial ventures forward.

Technology has become a cornerstone of modern entrepreneurship, enabling startups and small businesses to compete on a global scale, streamline operations, and deliver innovative products and services to customers. From artificial intelligence and blockchain to the Internet of Things (IoT) and cloud computing, a myriad of technologies are reshaping how entrepreneurs approach business challenges and seize opportunities in today's digital age.

In this chapter, we delve into the diverse ways in which entrepreneurs can harness technology to fuel their success. From leveraging data analytics and automation to optimize processes and enhance decision-making, to embracing digital marketing and e-commerce to reach new markets and engage customers, we explore the myriad of ways in which technology can drive growth and innovation within entrepreneurial ventures.

Moreover, we examine how emerging technologies such as augmented reality, virtual reality, and 3D printing are opening up new frontiers for entrepreneurship, enabling entrepreneurs to create immersive experiences, customize products, and disrupt traditional industries in novel ways.

As we embark on this exploration of technology-driven entrepreneurship, prepare to discover the tools, strategies, and best practices that can empower you to leverage technology as a catalyst for success in your entrepreneurial journey. Whether you're a seasoned entrepreneur or just starting, the insights and lessons shared in this chapter will equip you with the knowledge and inspiration needed to harness the power of technology and unlock new opportunities for growth and innovation in your venture.

- Leveraging Emerging Technologies to Drive Innovation

Emerging technologies hold immense potential to drive innovation and transform industries. In this section, we explore the process of leveraging emerging technologies to foster innovation within entrepreneurial ventures. From artificial intelligence and blockchain to virtual reality and 3D printing, we delve into how entrepreneurs can harness these cutting-edge technologies to create value, disrupt markets, and stay ahead of the competition.

1. Identify Relevant Emerging Technologies:

The first step in leveraging emerging technologies is to identify those that are most relevant to your industry, business model, and strategic objectives. Entrepreneurs must stay abreast of technological trends and advancements, conduct market research, and assess the potential impact of emerging technologies on their ventures. By understanding the capabilities and applications of emerging technologies, entrepreneurs can identify opportunities for innovation and competitive differentiation.

2. Experiment and Pilot Projects:

Once relevant emerging technologies have been identified, entrepreneurs should conduct experiments and pilot projects to explore their potential applications and feasibility within their venture. This may involve developing proof-of-concept prototypes, conducting small-scale trials, or collaborating with technology partners and experts.

By experimenting with emerging technologies in a controlled environment, entrepreneurs can gain valuable insights, test assumptions, and refine their innovation strategies.

3. Foster a Culture of Learning and Adaptation:

Leveraging emerging technologies requires a culture of learning, experimentation, and adaptation within the organization. Entrepreneurs must create an environment where employees feel empowered to explore new ideas, take calculated risks, and embrace change. By providing training, resources, and support for skill development, entrepreneurs can cultivate a workforce that is equipped to leverage emerging technologies effectively and drive innovation forward.

4. Collaborate with Technology Partners and Experts:

Entrepreneurs may not have the expertise or resources to develop and implement emerging technologies on their own. Collaboration with technology partners, startups, research institutions, and industry experts can provide access to specialized knowledge, resources, and capabilities needed to accelerate innovation. By forming strategic partnerships and alliances, entrepreneurs can leverage external expertise and networks to overcome barriers and capitalize on emerging opportunities.

5. Embrace Agile Development and Iterative Processes:

The rapid pace of technological change requires entrepreneurs to adopt agile development and iterative processes for innovation. Instead of pursuing large-scale, monolithic projects, entrepreneurs should break down initiatives into smaller, manageable tasks and iterate on solutions based on feedback and insights. By adopting an agile mindset and embracing iterative processes, entrepreneurs can adapt to evolving market conditions, minimize risk, and maximize the impact of their innovation efforts.

6. Monitor Trends and Evolve Strategy:

Leveraging emerging technologies is an ongoing process that requires monitoring trends, evolving strategies, and staying agile in response to changes in the technological landscape. Entrepreneurs must continuously scan the horizon for new developments, assess their implications for their venture, and adjust their innovation strategies accordingly. By staying proactive and nimble, entrepreneurs can position themselves to capitalize on emerging opportunities and maintain a competitive edge in the market.

Leveraging emerging technologies to drive innovation is essential for entrepreneurial ventures seeking to stay ahead of the curve and create value in today's fast-paced business environment. By identifying relevant emerging technologies, experimenting and piloting projects, fostering a culture of learning and adaptation, collaborating with technology partners and experts, embracing agile development and iterative processes, and monitoring trends to evolve strategy, entrepreneurs can harness the transformative power of technology to drive sustainable growth and success in their ventures.

- Integrating Digital Tools for Efficiency and Growth

In today's digital age, the strategic integration of digital tools is essential for entrepreneurs seeking to drive efficiency, streamline operations, and fuel growth within their ventures. From project management and communication tools to customer relationship management (CRM) systems and data analytics platforms, digital tools offer myriad opportunities to optimize processes, enhance productivity, and unlock new opportunities for innovation. In this section, we explore the comprehensive process of integrating digital tools for efficiency and growth within entrepreneurial ventures.

1. Assess Business Needs and Goals:

The first step in integrating digital tools is to assess the specific needs and goals of the business. Entrepreneurs must identify pain points, inefficiencies, and opportunities for improvement within their operations. This may involve conducting a thorough audit of existing processes, gathering feedback from stakeholders, and aligning digital initiatives with strategic objectives. By understanding the unique challenges and priorities of the business, entrepreneurs can make informed decisions about which digital tools to integrate and how to prioritize implementation efforts.

2. Research and Select Appropriate Tools:

Once business needs and goals have been identified, entrepreneurs should research and evaluate digital tools that align with their requirements and budget. This may involve exploring a wide range of options, reading reviews, and seeking recommendations from peers or industry experts. Entrepreneurs should consider factors such as functionality, scalability, ease of use, integration capabilities, and cost when selecting digital tools. By conducting thorough research and due diligence, entrepreneurs can choose tools that are well-suited to their specific needs and objectives.

3. Implement and Customize Tools:

After selecting digital tools, entrepreneurs must implement and customize them to fit the unique workflows and processes of their businesses. This may involve setting up accounts, configuring settings, and integrating tools with existing systems and platforms. Entrepreneurs should consider involving key stakeholders in the implementation process to ensure buy-in and alignment with organizational goals. Additionally, entrepreneurs may need to provide training and support to employees to facilitate adoption and maximize the benefits of the new tools.

4. Streamline Workflows and Automate Processes:

Digital tools offer opportunities to streamline workflows and automate repetitive tasks, saving time and resources for entrepreneurs. Entrepreneurs should identify manual processes that can be automated using digital tools, such as data entry, email marketing, invoicing, and project management. By automating routine tasks, entrepreneurs can free up valuable time to focus on strategic initiatives and value-added activities that drive growth.

5. Monitor Performance and Iterate:

Once digital tools have been integrated into the business, entrepreneurs should continuously monitor their performance and effectiveness. This may involve tracking key metrics, gathering feedback from users, and conducting regular reviews to assess the impact of digital initiatives on efficiency and growth. Based on insights gained from monitoring, entrepreneurs should be prepared to iterate and refine their digital strategies over time. By embracing a culture of continuous improvement, entrepreneurs can optimize the use of digital tools to drive ongoing efficiency and growth within their ventures.

6. Stay Agile and Adapt to Change:

In today's fast-paced business environment, entrepreneurs must stay agile and adapt to changes in technology, market conditions, and customer preferences. This may require regularly evaluating and updating digital toolsets to ensure they remain aligned with evolving business needs and objectives. Entrepreneurs should remain vigilant for emerging trends and innovations in digital technology, and be prepared to pivot their strategies accordingly. By staying agile and responsive to change, entrepreneurs can leverage digital tools as dynamic assets that support ongoing efficiency and growth within their ventures.

Integrating digital tools for efficiency and growth is a multifaceted process that requires careful planning, implementation, and ongoing management. By assessing business needs and goals, researching and selecting appropriate tools, implementing and customizing tools to fit workflows, streamlining processes, monitoring performance, and staying agile and adaptable, entrepreneurs can harness the transformative power of digital technology to drive efficiency and fuel growth within their ventures. Through strategic integration and optimization of digital tools, entrepreneurs can unlock new opportunities for innovation, differentiation, and success in today's digital-driven economy.

- Balancing Human Touch with Technological Advancements

In today's digital age, the strategic integration of digital tools is essential for entrepreneurs seeking to drive efficiency, streamline operations, and fuel growth within their ventures. From project management and communication tools to customer relationship management (CRM) systems and data analytics platforms, digital tools offer myriad opportunities to optimize processes, enhance productivity, and unlock new opportunities for innovation. In this section, we explore the comprehensive process of integrating digital tools for efficiency and growth within entrepreneurial ventures.

1. Assess Business Needs and Goals:

The first step in integrating digital tools is to assess the specific needs and goals of the business. Entrepreneurs must identify pain points, inefficiencies, and opportunities for improvement within their operations. This may involve conducting a thorough audit of existing processes, gathering feedback from stakeholders, and aligning digital initiatives with strategic objectives. By understanding the unique challenges and priorities of the business, entrepreneurs can make informed decisions about which digital tools to integrate and how to prioritize implementation efforts.

2. Research and Select Appropriate Tools:

Once business needs and goals have been identified, entrepreneurs should research and evaluate digital tools that align with their requirements and budget. This may involve exploring a wide range of options, reading reviews, and seeking recommendations from peers or industry experts. Entrepreneurs should consider factors such as functionality, scalability, ease of use, integration capabilities, and cost when selecting digital tools. By conducting thorough research and due diligence, entrepreneurs can choose tools that are well-suited to their specific needs and objectives.

3. Implement and Customize Tools:

After selecting digital tools, entrepreneurs must implement and customize them to fit the unique workflows and processes of their businesses. This may involve setting up accounts, configuring settings, and integrating tools with existing systems and platforms. Entrepreneurs should consider involving key stakeholders in the implementation process to ensure buy-in and alignment with organizational goals. Additionally, entrepreneurs may need to provide training and support to employees to facilitate adoption and maximize the benefits of the new tools.

4. Streamline Workflows and Automate Processes:

Digital tools offer opportunities to streamline workflows and automate repetitive tasks, saving time and resources for entrepreneurs. Entrepreneurs should identify manual processes that can be automated using digital tools, such as data entry, email marketing, invoicing, and project management. By automating routine tasks, entrepreneurs can free up valuable time to focus on strategic initiatives and value-added activities that drive growth.

5. Monitor Performance and Iterate:

Once digital tools have been integrated into the business, entrepreneurs should continuously monitor their performance and effectiveness. This may involve tracking key metrics, gathering feedback from users, and conducting regular reviews to assess the impact of digital initiatives on efficiency and growth. Based on insights gained from monitoring, entrepreneurs should be prepared to iterate and refine their digital strategies over time. By embracing a culture of continuous improvement, entrepreneurs can optimize the use of digital tools to drive ongoing efficiency and growth within their ventures.

6. Stay Agile and Adapt to Change:

In today's fast-paced business environment, entrepreneurs must stay agile and adapt to changes in technology, market conditions, and customer preferences. This may require regularly evaluating and updating digital toolsets to ensure they remain aligned with evolving business needs and objectives. Entrepreneurs should remain vigilant for emerging trends and innovations in digital technology, and be prepared to pivot their strategies accordingly. By staying agile and responsive to change, entrepreneurs can leverage digital tools as dynamic assets that support ongoing efficiency and growth within their ventures.

Integrating digital tools for efficiency and growth is a multifaceted process that requires careful planning, implementation, and ongoing management. By assessing business needs and goals, researching and selecting appropriate tools, implementing and customizing tools to fit workflows, streamlining processes, monitoring performance, and staying agile and adaptable, entrepreneurs can harness the transformative power of digital technology to drive efficiency and fuel growth within their ventures. Through strategic integration and optimization of digital tools, entrepreneurs can unlock new opportunities for innovation, differentiation, and success in today's digital-driven economy.

CONCLUSION

As we conclude our journey through "Innovate to Elevate: Unleashing Entrepreneurial Success," it's evident that innovation is the driving force behind entrepreneurial achievement in the ever-evolving landscape of business. Throughout this book, we've explored the transformative power of innovation, from fostering a culture of creativity and collaboration to harnessing emerging technologies and balancing the human touch with technological advancements.

Innovation isn't just about generating groundbreaking ideas; it's about embracing change, challenging the status quo, and relentlessly pursuing excellence in everything we do. It's about recognizing opportunities where others see obstacles, adapting to shifting market dynamics, and continuously evolving to stay ahead of the curve.

We've seen how successful entrepreneurs leverage innovation to disrupt industries, create value for customers, and drive sustainable growth. They embrace failure as a learning opportunity, pivot in response to feedback, and never lose sight of their vision for the future.

But innovation isn't a solitary pursuit—it's a collective endeavor that requires collaboration, diversity of thought, and a shared commitment to excellence. It's about empowering individuals to unleash their creative potential, fostering an environment where ideas flourish, and celebrating the successes that come from daring to dream big.

As you embark on your entrepreneurial journey, remember that innovation is not a destination—it's a mindset, a way of thinking and operating that propels you forward in the face of challenges and opportunities alike. Embrace uncertainty, embrace experimentation, and above all, embrace the belief that you have the power to shape the future through your ideas and actions.

So go forth, fellow innovators, and dare to innovate, dare to elevate, and dare to unleash your entrepreneurial success upon the world. The journey may be challenging, but the rewards are boundless for those who dare to dream, dare to innovate and dare to elevate themselves to new heights of achievement.